REAL-LIFE VAMPIRES

BLOODSUCKING MOSQUITOES

By Santana Hunt

 Gareth Stevens
PUBLISHING

Please visit our website, www.garethstevens.com. For a free color catalog of all our high-quality books, call toll free 1-800-542-2595 or fax 1-877-542-2596.

Library of Congress Cataloging-in-Publication Data

Hunt, Santana, author.
 Bloodsucking mosquitoes / Santana Hunt.
     pages cm. — (Real-life vampires)
 Includes bibliographical references and index.
ISBN 978-1-4824-3955-7 (pbk.)
ISBN 978-1-4824-3956-4 (6 pack)
ISBN 978-1-4824-3957-1 (library binding)
1. Mosquitoes—Juvenile literature. I. Title.
 QL536.H88 2016
 595.77'2—dc23
                                        2015021554

First Edition

Published in 2016 by
Gareth Stevens Publishing
111 East 14th Street, Suite 349
New York, NY 10003

Copyright © 2016 Gareth Stevens Publishing

Designer: Katelyn E. Reynolds
Editor: Kristen Nelson

Photo credits: Cover, p. 1 Anest/Shutterstock.com; cover, pp. 1–24 (background art) happykanppy/Shutterstock.com; p. 5 Coprid/Shutterstock.com; pp. 7, 9 BlueRingMedia/ Shutterstock.com; p. 11 claffra/Shutterstock.com; p. 13 Borkin Vadim; p. 15 Tim Boyle/Getty Images News/Getty Images; p. 17 David McNew/Getty Images News/Getty Images; p. 19 TONY KARUMBA/AFP/Getty Images; p. 21 (map) tovovan/Shutterstock.com; p. 21 (mosquito illustrations) Luciano Cosmo/Shutterstock.com.

Printed in the United States of America

CPSIA compliance information: Batch #CW16GS: For further information contact Gareth Stevens, New York, New York at 1-800-542-2595.

CONTENTS

Words in the glossary appear in **bold** type
the first time they are used in the text.

THAT AWFUL HUM!

On a hot summer evening, you might hear a familiar hum near your campfire or cookout—mosquitoes! The hum is the sound of their quickly beating wings getting closer and closer to you. Chances are good one is going to try to suck your blood—just like a **vampire**!

Mosquitoes are **insects** that need to take in blood to complete their life cycle. While that doesn't make batting them away any less bothersome, at least you'll soon know why they try to bite you!

FACT BITE

"Hematophagy" is the scientific word used for some animals' habit of drinking other animals' blood.

TINY BUG

Could you recognize a mosquito if you saw one? Mosquitoes have a thin body with three parts, six long legs, and two wings. Their head has two **compound eyes** and antennae with little hairs on them. The antennae help male mosquitoes "hear" the wingbeats of female mosquitoes.

Mosquitoes are only about 1/8 to 3/4 inch (0.3 to 1.9 cm) long and weigh almost nothing! You might not even notice one has landed on you until it's too late.

A mosquito's thorax connects to its head. Its legs and wings are also connected to the thorax. The abdomen houses many important **organs**, such as those that produce waste.

wings

thorax

antennae

abdomen

eyes

legs

proboscis

FROM EGG TO ADULT

Mosquito eggs are laid on the surface of water. Sometimes they gather in little bunches that float on the water. When mosquito larvae **hatch**, they're called "wigglers" because they move through the water by wiggling! Larvae **molt** several times and then become pupae, which also live in water. They remain in the water for 1 to 4 days.

Pupae form a case around themselves in which they turn into adult mosquitoes. Adult mosquitoes quickly look for a **mate**. Soon after, the bloodsucking begins!

Adult mosquitoes eat plant nectar, a sweet liquid plants make.

The Life Cycle of a Mosquito

adult mosquito

mosquito eggs

mosquito larva (wiggler)

mosquito pupa

TAKE A BITE!

Only female mosquitoes take in the blood of other animals. They have a special mouthpart called a proboscis (proh-BAH-suhs) that's very sharp. That's what they stick into your arm and suck your blood through!

But female mosquitoes aren't after blood for food. They need the **proteins** found in blood to fully **develop** their eggs. After they take in enough blood, female mosquitoes can lay their eggs. They need a fresh meal of blood each time they're preparing to lay eggs.

Female mosquito saliva contains anticoagulants, or matter that keeps blood flowing from a wound.

FACT BITE
The red, itchy bump caused by a mosquito bite is your body's **reaction** to the mosquito's saliva, or spit.

HOW DO THEY FIND ME?

Does it seem like mosquitoes are always able to find you when you're outside? That's because they can! Mosquitoes have developed ways of finding **prey** so they can suck their blood.

Mosquitoes can sense carbon dioxide, the gas many animals give off when they breathe out. They can also sense the body heat of nearby prey. Lastly, mosquitoes can *see* you! They notice colors and movement and guess there's something alive nearby that's full of needed blood.

Acting like a vampire is an important part of the mosquito life cycle!

DEATH AND DISEASE

There are more than 3,000 species, or kinds, of mosquitoes on Earth. All kinds of mosquitoes are bloodsuckers, but only a few hundred species take in blood from people. There are three groups of mosquitoes that cause the most trouble for people.

Mosquitoes in the groups *Anopheles*, *Culex*, and *Aedes* all act as vectors for deadly diseases, or illnesses. A vector is something that carries and gives a disease to an animal. Because they're disease carriers, mosquitoes are the deadliest animals on Earth.

FACT BITE
Millions of people die every year from diseases carried by mosquitoes.

Scientists called entomologists (ehn-tuh-MAH-luh-juhsts) study insects. They learn about mosquitoes to try to stop them from carrying diseases.

CARRIERS

In many places, a mosquito bite or two causes problems much worse than an itch. Mosquitoes begin carrying diseases after sucking the blood of prey that has the disease. It's then passed to the next person or animal they bite.

Culex mosquitoes carry a disease that causes a lot of pain and makes body parts get very large. *Aedes* mosquitoes are vectors for yellow fever, an illness that may cause someone to bleed from the mouth or nose. Both kinds carry a disease called West Nile virus.

FACT BITE

Midges are another kind of bloodsucking insect. One kind sucks the blood of mosquitoes! Midges can carry diseases, too.

MALARIA

Anopheles mosquitoes are perhaps the scariest disease carriers. They're vectors for malaria, among other illnesses. Malaria most often affects people who live where it's hot and wet, such as parts of Africa and Central America. More than half a million people died from malaria in 2013.

The mosquitoes that carry malaria commonly bite people at night. Many groups raise money to buy mosquito netting for people who live in areas with malaria-carrying mosquitoes. They cover their beds with it to keep the bloodsuckers out!

Some species of *Anopheles* like taking in human blood the best. That makes them likely to carry malaria between people.

FACT BITE

Malaria is caused by four species of **parasites** that grow inside *Anopheles* mosquitoes. Malaria gives people chills and fever.

SHOULD THEY BE STOPPED?

Scientists and people concerned about diseases around the world wonder if it would be better to get rid of some species of mosquitoes altogether! However, mosquitoes are prey for lots of fish and other animals. Without them, some habitats might become out of balance.

The best way to keep mosquitoes away is to stop them from laying eggs near where you live. Don't let standing water build up in your yard, including in rain buckets and ponds.

FACT BITE

If you have a mosquito bite, wash it with soap and water. Some medicated creams will help stop the itching.

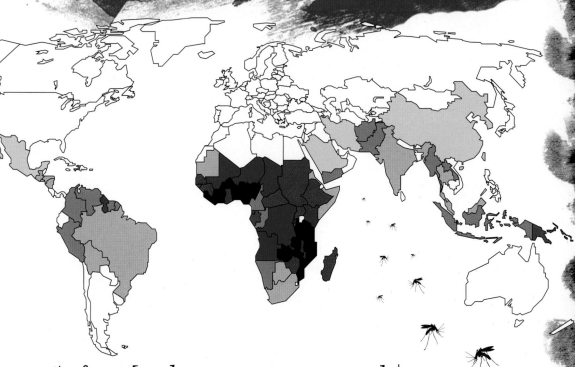

2014 WORLD MALARIA REPORT

Confirmed malaria cases per 1,000 population

- more than 100
- 50-100
- 10-50
- 1-10
- 0.1-1
- 0-0.1
- no ongoing malaria problem

GLOSSARY

compound eye: an eye that has many parts

develop: to grow and change

habitat: the natural place where an animal or plant lives

hatch: to come out of

insect: a small, often winged, animal with six legs and three main body parts

mate: one of two animals that come together to produce babies

molt: to shed an outer skeleton that has become too small

organ: a part inside an animal's body

parasite: a living thing that lives in, on, or with another living thing and often harms it

prey: animals hunted by other animals for food

protein: structural matter made by the body

reaction: the way something responds

vampire: a made-up being who drinks human blood

FOR MORE INFORMATION

Books

Carr, Aaron. *Mosquitoes*. New York, NY: AV2 by Weigl, 2016.

Rake, Jody Sullivan. *Bloodsuckers of the Animal World*. North Mankato, MN: Capstone Press, 2015.

Veitch, Catherine. *Learning About Insects*. Chicago, IL: Raintree, 2014.

Websites

Blood-Eating Animals
www.nwf.org/Kids/Ranger-Rick/Animals/Mixture-of-Species/Blood-Eating-Animals.aspx
Can't get enough bloodsuckers? Find more here!

Mosquito
kids.nationalgeographic.com/animals/mosquito/
Learn lots more about mosquitoes and their search for blood.

INDEX